Basic Skills Series

CAUSE & EFFECT

Using causes and effects to make connections

by
Karen Clemens Warrick

Cover Artist
Laura Zarrin

Illustrator
Susan Banta

Published by Instructional Fair • TS Denison
an imprint of

 McGraw-Hill
Children's Publishing

About the Author

Karen Clemens Warrick holds a bachelor's degree in science from Ball State University and a master's degree in elementary education from Arizona State University. After fifteen years of teaching, Karen became an author of both educational materials and biographies for children. She is a member of the Society of Children's Book Writers and Illustrators and has conducted writing workshops for teachers. Karen lives with her husband Jim in Prescott, Arizona.

Credits

Author: Karen Clemens Warrick

Cover Artist: Laura Zarrin

Cover Design: Matthew Van Zomeren

Inside Illustrations: Susan Banta

Project Director/Editor: Sara Bierling

Editors: Kathryn Wheeler, Susan Threatt

Graphic Layout: Tracy L. Wesorick

McGraw-Hill
Children's Publishing
A Division of The McGraw·Hill Companies

Published by Instructional Fair • TS Denison
An imprint of McGraw-Hill Children's Publishing
Copyright © 1999 McGraw-Hill Children's Publishing

Send all inquiries to:
McGraw-Hill Children's Publishing
3195 Wilson Drive NW
Grand Rapids, Michigan 49544

Cause & Effect—grades 1–2
ISBN: 0-7424-0099-9

About the Book

The activities included in this workbook provide teachers with tools for instruction and practice with recognizing cause and effect. Stories and informational writing makes more sense when readers understand why things happen and what makes them happen. Young readers will benefit from lessons that help them recognize stated cause and effect relationships within a sentence, across two sentences, and within a short paragraph. An introduction to cause and effect clue words is also helpful. The activities in *Cause & Effect* for grades 1–2 allow students to progress from recognizing cause and effect in art and in writing to writing cause and effect statements. Not only are these skills valuable for reading comprehension, but they also help students understand that actions have consequences.

Table of Contents

Name _____

Pack the Bags

We pack things because we need them.
Cut out the pictures below. Paste them in the right boxes.

1. Jody is going to camp. What should she put in her bag?	2. Jody is going to school. What should she put in her bag?

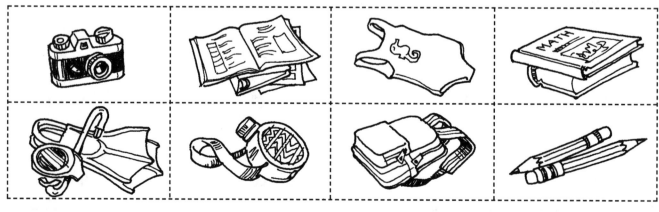

How Would You Feel?

What makes you feel happy or sad?
Circle the face that goes with each picture.

Cause   **Effect**

1.

2.

3.

4.

5.

Good Dog, Bad Dog

Look at the pictures. What made Kelly say, "Good dog!"?
What made him say, "Bad dog!"? Draw a line from the pictures
to the boxes to show what Kelly should say.

 "Good Dog!"

 "Bad Dog!"

Seasons

Seasons cause changes in nature.
Number the effects below using 1, 2, and 3.

1.

   _____   _____   _____

2.

   _____   _____   _____

3.

   _____   _____   _____

Try this: Make up your own sequence. Pick a plant or animal and show how it changes. You may also want to show why it changes.

Just for Fun!

The materials you have affect what you can create. Look at the picture sentences. Cut and paste the pictures below to show what you could make.

Cause   **Effect**

1. + + =

2.  + +  =

3.  =

4.  +  + =

5.  +  +  + =

   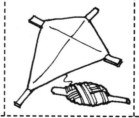 

What to Wear?

Look at each weather symbol. Circle what you should wear.

Cause	Effect

1.

2.

3.

4.

Time to Eat!

Look at each clock.
Circle the foods you would eat at that time.

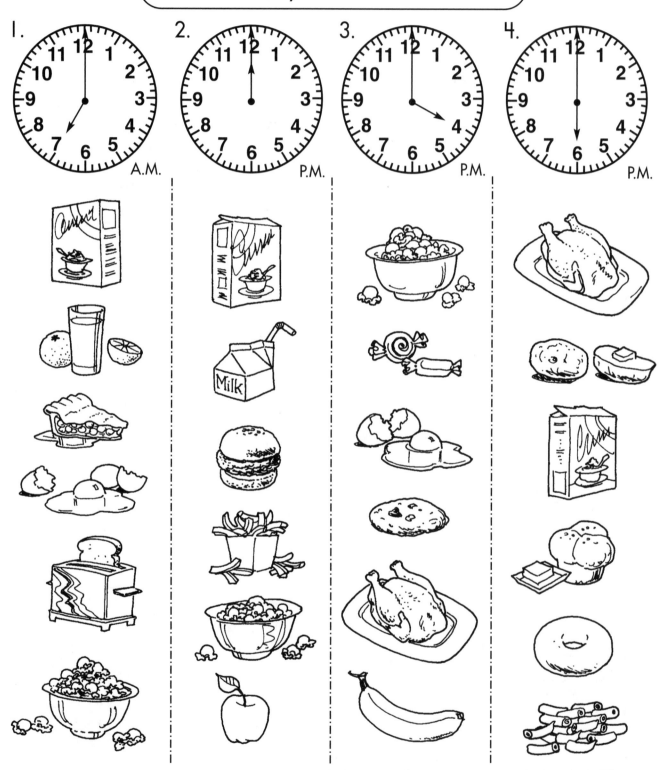

What Would You Say?

The effect is what happens. The cause is why it happened.
Match the cause with the effect by drawing a line.

Cause

1. "That ball is mine."

2. "Thank you Grandpa!"

3. "Oh, no!"

4. "Where did you go?"

5. "Stop!"

6. "Ow!"

7. "Can I have two scoops?"

ICE CREAM

Effect

a.

b.

c.

d.

e.

f.

g.

Color Mix-Up

What happens when you mix colors? Draw a line from the effect to the correct cause. Then follow the directions.

Effects

1. Color the trees green.

2. Color the sail on the boat purple.

3. Color the canoe orange.

Causes

a. blue and red

b. blue and yellow

c. red and yellow

4. Color the lake blue.   Color the sun yellow.   Color the dock red.

Adventure Park

North

Kim

Mary

Ramón

West  East

South

1. Kim is hot. He wants to cool off. He is going go to the:

   a. Petting Zoo   b. Fishing Pond   c. Swimming Hole

   Draw a red line to show how he will get there.

2. Mary wants to feed the goats. She is going to the:

   a. Petting Zoo   b. Fishing Pond   c. Swimming Hole

   Draw a blue line to show how she will get there.

3. Ramón got a new fishing pole. He is going to the:

   a. Petting Zoo   b. Fishing Pond   c. Swimming Hole

   Draw a green line to show how he will get there.

Temperatures

Read each weather report. Look at the thermometers.
Record the temperature on the line. Then circle what you should wear.

Cause   **Effect**

1. Monday will be sunny and warm.

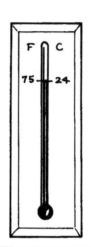

_____

2. Tuesday will be cooler.
   It will rain in the morning.

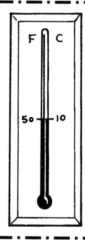

_____

3. Wednesday will be colder.
   The rain may turn to snow.

_____

What Makes Seeds Grow?

Read the story. Then answer the questions.

 helped and plant .

The children put dirt in a . Then they made a

hole in the dirt. They put three in the hole.

They covered the with dirt. They the

seeds. They put the ____ in a sunny ____ .

How seeds are cared for effects how they grow. Will Freda and Mike's seeds grow if:

1. Mike forgets to water his pot for a week?   **yes   no**

2. Freda waters her plant a little every day?   **yes   no**

3. Freda puts her pot in a dark closet?   **yes   no**

4. Mike puts his plant in a window in his room?   **yes   no**

5. Freda leaves her plant outside in cold weather?   **yes   no**

6. Circle the words that tell what seeds need to grow.

   sunlight   cold air   water   dirt   darkness

The Monkey and the Camel

Read the story. Then complete each sentence to tell the cause.

The zoo gave a party. It was the monkey's birthday. Everyone sang and danced. The monkey did tricks on the tightrope. All the animals clapped and cheered. His tricks were great. The camel wanted everyone to clap and cheer for him. The camel tried to walk the tightrope. The animals did not clap and cheer. The camel looked silly standing on the tightrope. Everyone laughed.

1. The zoo animals had a party because…

   a. it was fun.   b. it was the monkey's birthday.

2. The animals clapped and cheered for the monkey because…

   a. his tricks were great.   b. it was his birthday.

3. The animals laughed at the camel because…

   a. he looked so silly.   b. it was his birthday, too.

What Happened?

Can you guess what happened? Match the cause to the effect by writing the correct letter on the line.

Cause  **Effect**

___ 1. Kate was all wet because...

a. I threw his ball.

___ 2. John made a face because...

b. she was hot and thirsty.

___ 3. Joe's dad was mad because...

c. Joe forgot to put his bike away.

___ 4. My teacher smiled because...

d. I am hungry.

___ 5. My dog Scruff ran because...

e. she fell into the lake.

___ 6. Mike wanted Raquel on his team because...

f. his mom gave him ice cream.

___ 7. Keisha asked for a glass of water because...

g. the juice tasted funny.

___ 8. Toby smiled because...

h. she can hit the ball a long way.

___ 9. Everyone ran to the porch because...

i. we all did well in reading.

___ 10. I want some popcorn because...

j. it began to rain.

Sound Effects

Match the effect to the cause.

Effect

____1. Dusty ran to Jason…

____2. José lined up with the kids in his class…

____3. The soccer teams stopped playing…

____4. The man stopped his car…

____5. The cowboys picked up their plates and cups…

____6. The bank robber dropped the money and ran…

Cause

a. when the school bell rang.

b. when the policeman blew his whistle.

c. when the cook rang the dinner bell.

d. when Jason whistled for him.

e. when the alarm bell rang.

f. when the coach blew the whistle.

7. Who heard a whistle?

_____

_____

_____

8. Who heard a bell?

_____

_____

_____

In the News

Headlines tell what happened, or the *effect*. The news stories tell why it happened, or the *cause*. Write the correct headline above each story.

1. A baby elephant was born at the zoo on Monday. It weighed 95 pounds (43 kg).

Headline: _____

_____

2. The second grade students picked up litter after the school picnic. They will recycle the clean trash.

Headline: _____

_____

3. There had been no rain for weeks. Fireworks sparks set dry grass and bushes on fire.

Headline: _____

_____

4. Jeff pulled a drowning puppy out of his swimming pool. He is now looking for the puppy's owners.

Headline: _____

_____

5. Deb made a tent in her backyard. She used old newspaper for the walls. It was fun to play in the tent. Then the wind blew it away.

Headline: _____

_____

Headlines

Wind Blows House Down

Boy Saves Dog

Huge Baby Born

Fireworks Start Fire

Kids Clean Up

Silly Circus Parade

Read each story. Ask yourself, "What happened?" Draw one line under the effect. Then ask yourself, "Why?" Draw a circle around the cause.

1. The circus band rode in a wagon pulled by horses. The band had to jump off when one of the wheels fell off the wagon.

2. The elephants marched in a line. They held onto each other's tails. The first elephant sneezed and sat down. All the other elephants sat down, too.

3. The tall clown smelled the short clown's flower. Water squirted out of the flower. It hit the tall clown in the face. The tall clown chased the short clown down the street.

4. One monkey ate a banana. He threw the peel onto the street. The monkey trainer stepped on the peel. He slipped and fell.

That Could Not Happen!

Read the sentences. Could that really happen? Tell why or why not.

1. A bear wanted a chipmunk's nut, so it climbed into the chipmunk's nest.

   That could not happen because...

   a. chipmunks do not eat nuts.

   b. bears are too big.

2. Joe has tennis shoes with wings. That is why he can jump sky high.

   That could not happen because...

   a. Joe cannot jump.

   b. tennis shoes don't have wings.

3. The dish ran away with the spoon, so the little boy could not eat his supper.

   That could not happen because...

   a. the boy could use a fork.

   b. a dish and spoon cannot run.

4. A dragon knocked on my door. When I did not let it in, it burned down the door.

   That could not happen because...

   a. dragons are make-believe.

   b. dragons are friendly.

5. One ant carried a peanut-butter sandwich to the anthill. All the ants had a picnic.

   That could not happen because...

   a. one ant could not carry a sandwich.

   b. ants do not eat peanut butter.

Find the Clues

Clue words can help you find the cause and effect. Some clue words to look for are *because*, *so*, *when*, and *why*. Circle the clue words in the sentences below. Then write the cause and effect.

1. The clock broke when my dog knocked it off the table.

   Cause: _____

   Effect: _____

2. I forgot to mow the lawn, so I can not play.

   Cause: _____

   Effect: _____

3. I fell off my bike because my tire hit a rock.

   Cause: _____

   Effect: _____

4. Mom was mad when I laughed at my brother.

   Cause: _____

   Effect: _____

5. I ran away because the dog growled at me.

   Cause: _____

   Effect: _____

6. I am your friend because you are funny and nice.

   Cause: _____

   Effect: _____

Math Mistakes

Check each problem. What caused the mistake? Find the correct answer.

1. Carlos had 12 cookies. He gave 6 to Jeff. How many did Carlos have left?

   $12 + 6 = 18$

   wrong answer

The student got the wrong answer because:

a. He added wrong.

b. He needed to subtract.

The right answer is:_____

2. Amy had 6 shells. Kamal had 4 shells. Tracy had 5 shells. How many shells were there all together?

   $6 + 4 = 10$

   wrong answer

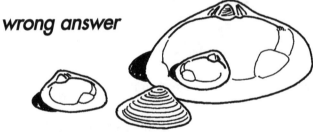

The student got the wrong answer because:

a. She subtracted.

b. She forgot to add one of the numbers.

The right answer is:_____

3. Tremel had a nickel and a dime. Nita had two dimes. How much more money did Nita have?

   $15¢ + 20¢ = 35¢$

   wrong answer

The student got the wrong answer because:

a. He added.

b. He subtracted.

The right answer is:_____

Glaciers

(Read the article. Then complete the sentences.)

Glaciers start high in the mountains where lots of snow falls. It stays cold high in the mountains. The snow does not melt. As more snow falls, the flakes pack together. This is like the way snow gets packed together to make a snowball. Snow gets packed so closely that ice forms. When more snow falls, the ice gets thicker and heavier. Then it begins to slide. The moving ice is called a glacier.

What happens? Match the cause to the effect.

_____ 1. When the ice gets thicker and heavier,

_____ 2. High in the mountains where it stays cold,

_____ 3. When the snow packs closely,

_____ 4. When more snow falls,

a. snow falls.

b. ice forms.

c. the snow packs together.

d. it begins to slide.

Try this: Number the sentences to show what happened first, second, third, and fourth.

Science Magic

> Read the story. Then complete the sentences below.

Joe shared a magic science trick with his class. He said, "How can you tell a raw egg from a hard-boiled egg without cracking it open?"

Marta asked, "Shake it?"

"No," said Joe. "Watch this. One of these eggs is hard-boiled. The other one is raw."

Joe put the eggs on the table. He made each egg spin like a top. Then he gently touched the top of each egg with two fingers. One egg stopped. The other one kept spinning. Joe picked up the egg that stopped spinning.

"This is the hard-boiled egg," Joe said. "The raw egg inside the shell keeps moving. That makes the raw egg keep spinning. The hard-boiled egg stops because nothing inside the shell is moving."

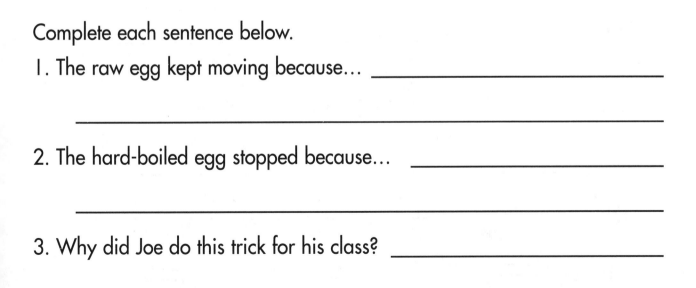

Complete each sentence below.

1. The raw egg kept moving because... _____

_____

2. The hard-boiled egg stopped because... _____

_____

3. Why did Joe do this trick for his class? _____

_____

Name _____

Pets

> Remember: To find the effect, ask yourself, "What happened?"
> To find the cause, ask yourself, "Why?"
> Write the cause, then write the effect.

1. Jody's dog jumped up and wagged its tail when Jody poured food into a dish.

   Cause: _____

   Effect: _____

2. Mary cried because her cat was stuck in the tree.

   Cause: _____

   Effect: _____

3. Greg's hamster climbed a toy ladder to get some cheese.

   Cause: _____

   Effect: _____

4. Amy walked to the barn. She had an apple in her hand. He pony ran to the fence.

   Cause: _____

   Effect: _____

Camping Out

Read the story. Then answer the questions below.

Karen and Jim were going camping with Dad. They loaded sleeping bags and a camp stove into the van. Mom filled a box with bread, peanut butter, cookies, apples, and chips. Dad carried out the ice chest and a jug of water.

"We are ready to go," he said.

When they got to the state park, Karen and Jim helped Dad set up camp.

"Bring me the tent," Dad said.

Jim looked in the van. "It's not here."

"Oh, no!" cried Karen. "We forgot the tent. We will have to go home."

"No," Dad said. "It's a nice, warm night. And it's not going to rain. We will roll our sleeping bags out on the ground. The sky will be our tent."

"Hurray!" shouted Karen and Jim.

1. Why did Karen think they would have to go home? _____

_____

_____

2. Why did they get to stay? _____

_____

_____

3. What did they use as a tent? _____

4. What do you think will happen if it rains? _____

_____

Letter to Grandma

Read the letter. Add any missing punctuation. Then answer the questions.

Dear Grandma

     I didn't go to school today because it snowed a lot. I wanted to go outside as soon as I woke up. Mom said it was too cold

     Later, I put on my jacket my mittens my hat and a scarf.

     I could not go sledding because I broke my sled. I made a snowman instead. Do you like to make snowmen I drew a picture of the snowman because it will melt soon. His eyes are pine cones. Can you guess what I used for a mouth

Love

Danny

Circle all the answers that are true.

1. It snowed, so Danny…

  a. didn't have to go to school.

  b. had to stay inside all day.

  c. could not go sledding.

  d. had to wear warm clothes.

  e. decided to make a snowman.

2. Danny put on a jacket, mittens, hat, and scarf…

  a. because it was cold outside.

  b. because he was going sledding.

  c. because he was going to play in the snow.

  d. because he wanted to see Grandma.

A Picnic

(Read the story. Then choose the best answers below.)

One sunny day, Mrs. Ant said, "Let's go to the park for a picnic."

"Good idea," said Mr. Ant. "Families will be eating there."

"Can we go now?" asked Art Ant. "I am hungry."

"I don't want to go," said Amy Ant.

"Why not?" asked Mrs. Ant.

"Last time we did not find any food," Amy said.

"This time we might find lots of food," said Art.

Everyone followed Mrs. Ant to the park. They walked under a picnic table. The four ants sat down. Then they all looked up. They waited.

1. The Ants went to the park for a picnic because…

   a. the park was pretty.

   b. families eat in the park.

2. Art Ant wanted to go because…

   a. he could play in the grass.

   b. he was hungry.

3. Amy Ant didn't want to go because…

   a. sometimes people don't leave food.

   b. sometimes people step on ants.

4. The Ant family sat under the picnic table and looked up…

   a. to watch the sky.

   b. to wait for food to drop down.

Vote for Me

Mrs. Miller is holding a class election to help her students learn about voting. Marissa and Trevor both decide to run for class president. Read the posters that tell what each will do. Then answer the questions below.

Vote for Marissa

I will get a pet for our room.

I think we should have art every Friday.

I want our class to read to the kindergarten class once a month.

We should get chocolate milk every day.

Vote for Trevor

I will ask Mrs. Miller to give homework only on Wednesdays.

We will play soccer every Friday.

I want the class to recycle paper.

We need more computer time.

1. Why is Mrs. Miller holding an election? _____

_____

2. John loves chocolate milk. He does not like soccer. He voted for   Marissa   Trevor

3. Mary does not like to draw. She is good on the computer. She voted for   Marissa   Trevor

4. Tina loves animals. She wants to be a vet. She voted for   Marissa   Trevor

5. Mason loves to read and draw. He voted for   Marissa   Trevor

Name _____

Vote For Me (cont.)

> Count the votes for Marissa and Trevor. Add the votes in each row.

Row	1	2	3	4	5	6

6. How many votes did Marissa get? _____

7. How many votes did Trevor get? _____

8. How many more votes did the winner get? _____

9. How many students voted? _____

10. For whom would you vote? _____ Why? _____

_____

> **Try this**: Design your own campaign poster. What will you do for your class and why?

 Name _____

Polly's Report Card

Polly walked home slowly after getting her report card. Look at the card. Then circle the best answer to the questions below.

Report Card

Reading	☆
Writing	☆
Spelling	☆
Math	☆

Gets along with others ☆

Follows directions ☹

Listens carefully ☹

Polly is a good student, but she talks too much.
Mrs. Mole

1. Polly walked home slowly because…

   a. she was proud of her report card.

   b. she was tired.

   c. Mama was not going to like what she read.

2. Mama will be proud of Polly because…

   a. she got five stars on her report card.

   b. she is a perfect student.

   c. her teacher likes Polly.

3. Mama will want Polly to…

   a. get along better with others.

   b. listen carefully and follow directions.

   c. practice her reading.

4. We know Polly is a good student because…

   a. Mrs. Mole said she was a good student.

   b. she gets along with others.

School Program

Read about what happened during a special school program. Then complete each statement.

_____

9:00 Students read tree poem.

9:05 Fifth graders plant four trees.

9:30 Fourth graders present "Why We Love Trees."

9:45 First graders present "Parade of Leaves."

10:00 Recess will be spent playing under the trees.

1. All the poetry books in the school library were checked out because…

   a. the students love poetry.

   b. students were reading tree poems.

2. The fifth graders dug four deep holes the day before the program so…

   a. they could plant four trees.

   b. they could jump in and out of them.

3. The first graders taped leaves on their shirts for their parade of trees so…

   a. they could look funny.

   b. they could look like trees.

4. All the events are about trees because this program is for…

   a. Arbor Day.

   b. May Day.

   c. Halloween.

5. Read the titles below. Write the best title at the top of the program.

   Today Is Arbor Day

   Trees Are Green

   Growing Trees

© *Instructional Fair • TS Denison*

33

IF5626 *Cause & Effect*

Two Little Pigs

Read the story.

Once upon a time there were two little pigs. They lived with their mother in the city. The two little pigs wanted to live in the country. They could plant a garden in the country. They would make new animal friends, too.

When they kissed their mother goodbye, she said, "Watch out for the wolf. Little pigs are his favorite snack."

The pigs walked until they found a pile of sticks. "I'm tired of walking. I will build a house with these sticks," said the first little pig. And he did.

The second little pig walked on until he saw a pile of stones. "I will build my house of stones and mud," he said, "because it will be strong."

When the hungry wolf heard about the two pigs, he went hunting for a tasty snack. He blew down the first pig's house with one huff because the stick house was not strong. The first little pig ran to his brother's house. The wolf followed him. But the wolf went home hungry that day. The two little pigs were safe inside the strong house of stone.

Two Little Pigs (cont.)

(Circle all the correct answers below.)

1. The little pigs wanted to move to the country because…

   a. they liked the wolf.

   b. they wanted to make new friends.

   c. they wanted to plant a garden.

2. The wolf was hungry. How did that affect the little pigs?

   a. He wanted to be their friend.

   b. He wanted to eat them as a snack.

   c. He wanted to show them how strong he was.

3. Why did the first pig build a house of sticks?

   a. Because the sticks were strong.

   b. Because he wanted to build the first house.

   c. Because he was tired of walking.

4. Why did the second pig build a house of stone and mud?

   a. Because he knew the house would be strong.

   b. Because he was afraid of the wolf.

   c. Because his brother used all the sticks.

5. Why did the pigs' mother warn them to watch out for the wolf?

   a. The wolf is ugly.

   b. Little pigs are the wolf's favorite snack.

   c. The wolf would help them.

6. Why did the wolf go home hungry?

   _____

   _____

   _____

   _____

   _____

   _____

Polly's Terrible Day

Read about Polly's terrible day. Remember what happened and why.
Circle the clue words (*because, why, when,* and *so*).

One warm spring day, Polly Packrat said, "I think I will go looking for things. I need more stuff to decorate my room."

Polly started down the forest trail. She took her wagon so she could put all the things she found in it. Polly looked to the left. She looked to the right. She looked up above her. She looked down at her feet. Then she saw a stack of bottle caps. She scooped them up and put them in her wagon.

"No, no! Don't take my bottle caps!" yelled Sammy Squirrel. "I am going to paste them on a picture for my teacher. That is why I have been saving them."

Polly walked down the path with her wagon. When she saw a stack of newspapers in front of Rick Raccoon's den, she asked, "Do you need all these papers, Mr. Raccoon?"

"I am saving them so I can start warm fires this winter. I need them," he said.

Polly was sad because she wanted the papers, too. She walked on. Soon she saw some pretty flowers. She decided to pick them for her mother because her mother loved flowers.

Polly started to pick a flower. Then a bee buzzed by. "Please do not pick the flowers. We bees need the flowers so we can make honey."

Sadly, Polly turned to go home with her empty wagon. Mama opened the front door just as she got there.

"Where have you been?" she asked.

Then she saw Polly's empty wagon. Mama smiled a big smile because she was happy. Polly had not come home with more trash.

Polly's Terrible Day (cont.)

(Answer the questions below.)

1. Why did Polly take her wagon? _____

_____

2. Why had Sammy saved the bottle caps? _____

_____

3. Why did Rick Raccoon need the papers? _____

_____

4. Why did the bee need the flowers? _____

_____

5. What made Mama smile? _____

_____

Draw a line to show where Polly went on her treasure hunt.

Name _____

Write On!

Read the sentence groups below. Write one sentence that shows both the cause and effect. Use a clue word (*because*, *so*, *why*, or *when*) in your sentence.

1. Tony spilled his milk.
   Mom got mad.

_____

_____

2. The big black dog barked at Tina.
   She ran home crying.

_____

_____

3. The little bird could not get back to its nest.
   It could not fly.

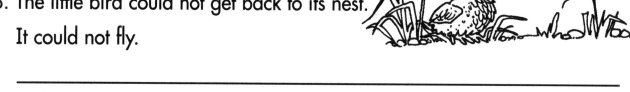

_____

_____

4. Joan kicked the ball into the street.
   She ran to tell the teacher.

_____

_____

Name _____

Chain Reaction

Read the story. Then complete the activity.

Terri dropped the marble. It hit the sleeping cat on the nose. The surprised cat jumped on the dog's tail. The dog yipped and chased the cat. The cat ran under the fish tank. The fish tank wobbled back and forth. Water and one small fish splashed out onto the floor. The happy cat ate the fish. The thirsty dog lapped up the water.

What happened:

1. First: _____

2. Second: _____

3. Third: _____

4. Fourth: _____

5. Fifth: _____

6. Sixth: _____

7. Seventh: _____

8. Eighth: _____

9. Ninth: _____

10. What caused the chain reaction? _____

_____

_____

The Food Chain

Read the article. Then complete the activity.

Predators are animals that eat other animals. The animals they eat are called **prey**. Predators and prey do important jobs in nature. Prey animals are food for the animals that hunt them. But predators also help prey. For example, coyotes hunt rabbits. If coyotes did not eat some rabbits, there would be too many rabbits hopping around. There would not be enough food for all the rabbits to eat. Then the hungry rabbits would grow weak and sick. Some might even die.

Use **predators** or **prey** to complete each sentence.

1. Coyotes are called _____ because they eat other animals.

2. Rabbits are called _____ because they are animals that coyotes and rattlesnakes eat.

3. If some _____ animals did not get eaten by _____, there would be too many animals and too little food.

4. Draw arrows between the words to show the food chain.

plants   rabbits   coyotes

The Food Chain Game

Mrs. Jones's class played a food chain game.
Read the story and look at the chart. Then answer the questions.

Mrs. Jones gave each student a large paper bag. The students put the paper bags with holes cut in them over their heads. When Mrs. Jones blew the whistle, each child made the sound of one of these animals: coyote, roadrunner, rabbit, rattlesnake, and lizard. Each predator or prey had to try to survive without being eaten. She reminded students to listen carefully to the sounds around them.

At the end of the game, these are the animals that were still alive: all the coyotes, 2 roadrunners, 0 rattlesnakes, 0 rabbits, and 1 lizard.

1. Why do you think all the coyotes were still alive?

   _____

   _____

2. Why had all the rattlesnakes and rabbits been caught?

   a. Two kinds of predators could catch them.

   b. They moved too slowly.

3. Why did Mrs. Jones have her class play this game?

   _____

   _____

   _____

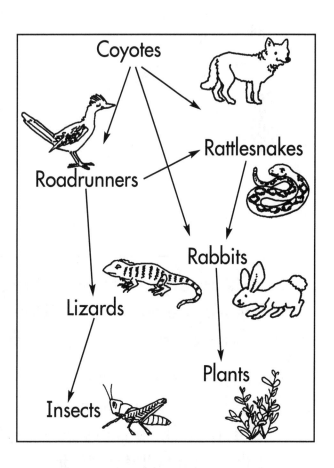

Deserts on the Map

> Look at the map. Read the article.
> Then answer the questions on page 43.

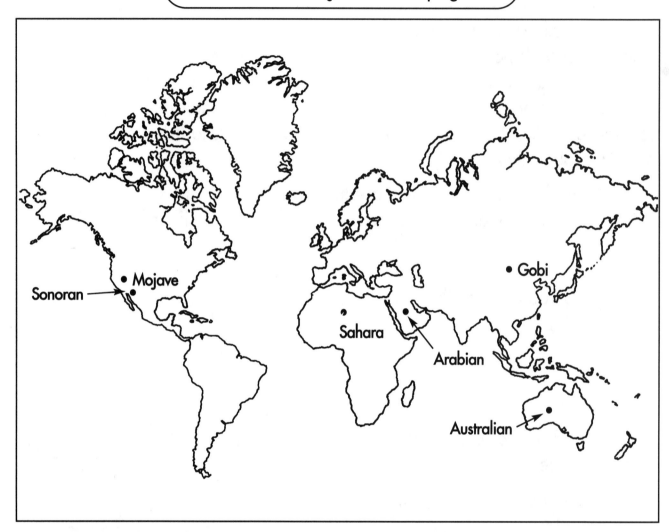

Deserts are dry places that get less than 10 inches (25 cm) of rain every year. The Mojave and Sonoran Deserts are found in a rain shadow. This means that most rain falls on the side of the mountains away from the desert.

The largest deserts in the world are the Sahara, the Australian, and the Arabian deserts. They are near the equator where it is very hot and dry. The Gobi Desert in China is dry because little moisture from the ocean reaches the air there. Not all deserts are hot. Some deserts are places where it is too cold for plants to grow.

Name _____

Deserts on the Map (cont.)

Answer the questions below.

1. When a place gets less than 10 inches (25 cm) of rainfall, it is called a...

   a. desert.

   b. hot, dry spot.

   c. rain shadow.

2. Write the names of three deserts that exist because they are close to the equator.

   _____   _____   _____

3. Write the names of two deserts caused by mountain rain shadows.

   _____   _____

4. Why is the Gobi a desert?

   a. The desert has mountains all around it.

   b. It is near the equator.

   c. It does not get much moisture from the ocean.

   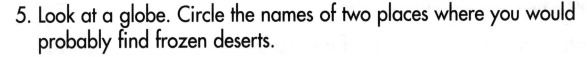

5. Look at a globe. Circle the names of two places where you would probably find frozen deserts.

   a. Antarctica

   b. Hawaii

   c. Greenland

Sky Watch

Read each part of the story. Write a sentence that summarizes what happened and why.

1. Trish put on her hat and coat. "I'm going to the library," she said to her mom.

    "Why?" her mom asked.

    "I'm doing a project for the school science fair. It's about stars. I need a book so I can plan my report."

    The librarian showed Trish where to look for books about stars. She found three books and checked them out.

    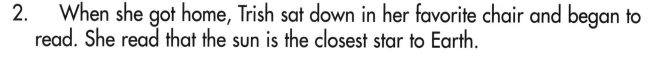

2. When she got home, Trish sat down in her favorite chair and began to read. She read that the sun is the closest star to Earth.

    "Hey, Mom," Trish said. "Did you know that our sun is a star?"

    "It's a very important star," Mom said.

    Trish made a poster of the sun for her star project.

    _____

    _____

    _____

3.   Trish lived in the big city. One clear night, she went out in her backyard and looked up at the sky. She tried to count the stars. They were hard to count because of all the city lights.

   "Mom, where can I see lots and lots of stars?" she asked.

   "You can see stars when we go to Grandpa's house," Mom told her.

   "When can we go?" Trish asked.

_____

_____

_____

4.   The next Saturday, Mom and Trish drove to Grandpa's house. He lived out in the country on the top of a hill. There were no houses or stores near his house.

   "Grandpa," Trish said. "Mom said I would see lots of stars here."

   Grandpa looked up at the sky. "There are no clouds tonight, so we will see lots of stars. I have a special surprise for you, too."

   "What is it, Grandpa?" Trish cried.

   "Wait until it gets dark." Grandpa said.

   When they went outside after dark, Trish saw more stars than she could count. Then Grandpa showed Trish the surprise. It was a telescope that would help her see the stars even better.

_____

_____

_____

Answer Key

Pack the Bags...........................4
1. swim suit, snorkel and fins, camera, canteen
2. pencils, homework, text books, backpack

How Would You Feel?...........................5
1. happy
2. sad
3. sad
4. sad
5. happy

Good Dog, Bad Dog...........................6
Good Dog: dog bringing boy ball, dog chewing bone, dog sitting up
Bad Dog: dog digging, dog chewing shoe, dog running away, dog barking

Seasons...........................7
1. 1, 2, 3
2. 2, 1, 3
3. 1, 3, 2

Just for Fun!...........................8
1. sandwich
2. mask
3. kite
4. sandcastle
5. snowman

What to Wear?...........................9
1. mittens, boots, jacket
2. sweater, pants, shoes
3. shorts, sunglasses, sun hat
4. raincoat, umbrella, rain boots

Time to Eat!...........................10
1. cereal, juice, eggs, toast
2. milk, hamburger, fries, apple

3. popcorn, candy, cookie, banana
4. chicken, potato, roll, green beans

What Would You Say?...........................11
1. c
2. d
3. a
4. b
5. g
6. f
7. e

Color Mix-Up...........................12
1. b
2. a
3. c
4. Picture should be colored appropriately.

Adventure Park...........................13
1. c
2. a
3. b

Temperatures...........................14
1. 75° F or 24° C, t-shirt and shorts
2. 50° F or 10° C, raincoat and umbrella
3. 30° F or -1 ° C, scarf, mittens, and hat

What Makes Seeds Grow?...........................15
1. no
2. yes
3. no
4. yes
5. no
6. sunlight, water, dirt

The Monkey and the Camel...........................16
1. b
2. a
3. a

What Happened?...........................17
1. e
2. g
3. c
4. i
5. a
6. h
7. b
8. f
9. j
10. d

Sound Effects...........................18
1. d
2. a
3. f
4. b
5. c
6. e
7. Dusty, the soccer teams, man in the car
8. José, the cowboys, the bank robber

In the News...........................19
1. Huge Baby Born
2. Kids Clean Up
3. Fireworks Start Fire
4. Boy Saves Dog
5. Wind Blows House Down

Silly Circus Parade...........................20
1. band had to jump off
   one of the wheels fell off the wagon.
2. All the other elephants sat

down, too.

> The first elephant sneezed and sat down.

3. The tall clown chased the short clown down the street.

> Water squirted out of the flower. It hit the tall clown in the face.

4. He slipped and fell.

> The monkey trainer stepped on the peel.

That Could Not Happen! 21

1. b
2. b
3. b
4. a
5. a

Find the Clues 22

1. **cause:** My dog knocked it off the table.
   effect: The clock broke.
2. **cause:** I forgot to mow the lawn.
   effect: I can not play.
3. **cause:** My tire hit a rock.
   effect: I fell off my bike.
4. **cause:** I laughed at my brother.
   effect: Mom was mad.
5. **cause:** The dog growled at me.
   effect: I ran away.
6. **cause:** You are funny and nice.
   effect: I am your friend.

Math Mistakes 23

1. b, 6
2. b, 15
3. a, 5¢

Glaciers 24

1. d
2. a
3. b
4. c

Science Magic 25

1. the egg inside kept moving.
2. nothing inside the shell was moving.
3. Answers will vary.

Pets 26

1. **cause:** Jody poured food into a dish.
   effect: His dog jumped up and wagged its tail.
2. **cause:** Her cat got stuck in the tree.
   effect: Mary cried.
3. **cause:** He wanted some cheese.
   effect: The hamster climbed a ladder.
4. **cause:** Amy had an apple.
   effect: The pony ran to the fence.

Camping Out 27

1. They left their tent behind.
2. Dad said they could sleep on the ground.
3. The sky was their tent.
4. Answers will vary.

Letter to Grandma 28

1. a, d, e
2. a, c

A Picnic 29

1. b
2. b
3. a

4. b

Vote for Me 30–31

1. Her students will learn about voting.
2. Marissa
3. Trevor
4. Marissa
5. Marissa
6. 14
7. 9
8. 5
9. 23
10. Answers will vary.

Polly's Report Card 32

1. c
2. a
3. b
4. a

School Program 33

1. b
2. a
3. b
4. a
5. Today Is Arbor Day

Two Little Pigs 34–35

1. b, c
2. b
3. c
4. a
5. b
6. He couldn't blow down the stone house and eat the pigs.

Polly's Terrible Day 36–37

1. She could carry all that she found.
2. He wanted to make a picture for his teacher.
3. He needed papers to make

warm fires in winter.

4. Flowers help bees make honey.

5. Polly had not brought home any more junk.

Answers will vary.

Possible answers are:

1. Mom got mad because Tony spilled his milk.

2. The big black dog barked at Tina, so she ran home crying.

3. The little bird could not get back to its nest because it could not fly.

4. Joan kicked the ball into the street, so she ran to tell the teacher.

1. Terri dropped the marble.

2. It hit the cat.

3. The cat jumped on the dog.

4. The dog chased the cat.

5. The cat ran under the fish tank.

6. The fish tank wobbled.

7. Water and a fish fell on the floor.

8. The cat ate the fish.

9. The dog drank the water.

10. Terri dropped a marble on the cat's nose.

1. predators

2. prey

3. prey, predators

4. plants → rabbits → coyotes

1. They are the biggest

predators. They are at the top of the food chain.

2. a

3. She wanted her class to understand the food chain.

1. a

2. Sahara, Australian, Arabian

3. Mojave, Sonoran

4. c

5. a, c

Answers will vary.

Possible answers are:

1. Trish went to the library because she needed books for her report on stars.

2. Trish made a poster about the sun because it is a star.

3. Trish could not count the stars because the city lights made them hard to see.

4. Grandpa and Trish used a telescope so they could see the stars better.